THE WORLD OF NASCAR

DIRT TRACK DAREDEVILS:
The History of NASCAR

TRADITION BOOKS™
EXCELSIOR, MINNESOTA

BY BOB WOODS

Published by **Tradition Books**™ and distributed to the
school and library market by **The Child's World**®
P.O. Box 326
Chanhassen, MN 55317-0326
800/599-READ
http://www.childsworld.com

Photo Credits
Allsport: 25 top (Robert Laberge); 25 bottom (Jamie Squire)
AP/Wide World: 9, 17, 18, 20, 21, 22, 26
Sports Gallery: 6, 24, 28 (2) (Brian Spurlock); 23, 27 (Joe Robbins)

The following photos are the exclusive property of ISC Publications-Archives, © ISC
Publications. All rights reserved. Used with permission: Cover and title page, 5, 10, 11, 13, 14, 15

Book production by Shoreline Publishing Group, LLC
Art direction and design by The Design Lab

Library of Congress Cataloging-in-Publication Data

Woods, Bob.
  Dirt track daredevils : the history of NASCAR / by Bob Woods.
    p. cm. — (The world of NASCAR series)
Summary: Surveys important people and events throughout the history of NASCAR. Includes
bibliographical references and index.
  ISBN 1-59187-004-6
  1. NASCAR (Association)—History—Juvenile literature. 2. Stock car racing—United
States—History—Juvenile literature. [1. NASCAR (Association)—History. 2. Stock car
racing—History.] I. Title: History of NASCAR. II. Title. III. Series.
  GV1029.9.S74 W66 2002   2002004643

DIRT TRACK DAREDEVILS

Table of Contents

INTRODUCTION

Fifty Years of Speed

NASCAR is an action-packed, colorful, star-studded show. From the historic oval track at Daytona Beach, Florida, to the twisty road course at Sears Point, California, stock car racing has taken the United States by storm.

The sport has always been about fast cars and the dare-devils who drive them. NASCAR wasn't always such a big show, however. Racing everyday automobiles—or stock cars—rather than specially built race cars started in the South during the 1930s. "Good ol' boys," skilled at outrunning the police over back roads, challenged each other. At first, races were run on crude dirt tracks. Rules were few and prize money was scarce, although the crowds kept cheering for more.

Then along came William France Sr. He loved stock car racing, but grew frustrated because it was so unorganized. In December 1947, Big Bill assembled a group of top drivers, promoters, and others. They agreed to form the National Association for Stock Car Automobile Racing (NASCAR). Before long, there were paved tracks up and down the east coast. The excitement quickly spread. Early superstars such as Lee Petty, Junior Johnson, and Fireball Roberts dueled for national championships.

By the 1960s and 1970s, big companies were sponsoring cars and drivers. Television began to broadcast big races.

Early race cars experimented with different designs, but with one goal: speed!

Richard Petty, David Pearson, and Cale Yarborough were among the new stars. In the 1980s and 1990s, Dale Earnhardt, Bill Elliott, Darrell Waltrip, Jeff Gordon, and others thrilled fans. In little more than half a century, NASCAR has gone from a rough and tumble beginning to a big-time sports phenomenon.

Today's stock cars are designed with the help of computers and are filled with safety gear.

CHAPTER ONE

Rough and Tumble Beginnings

How long have cars been racing? An old joke says they've been racing since the world's second car was built. That's not far from the truth. In 1901, early car maker Henry Ford beat fellow pioneer Alexander Winton in one of the very first car races.

One hundred years later, Ford's motor company is one of three automakers whose cars dominate NASCAR. General Motors and DaimlerChrysler also supply cars to this top stock car organization. Mr. Ford surely has something to do with it, but the real roots of NASCAR are firmly planted in the American South of the 1930s and 1940s.

"Roots" is the right word, because NASCAR's birth has a lot

to do with dirt. That's where people grew the corn, barley, rye, and yeast used to brew moonshine. Moonshine is an illegal alcoholic beverage popular during that period. Daring young men would load up the trunks of their cars with cases of moonshine. Then they would deliver it to secret locations, often in the Carolinas and Georgia. They sometimes had to escape government agents called revenuers, whose job was to arrest moonshiners. High-speed chases often would follow, typically over back-country dirt roads. The slick-driving moon-shine runners left the revenuers in their dust.

Before long, those "good ol' boys" challenged each other to friendly races along back roads. The action eventually shifted to oval dirt racetracks, which had sprung up across the country by the late 1940s. At the time, the established races included the Indianapolis 500 and **Grand Prix** events. The new type of auto racing was loosely organized, with few rules, minimal safety regulations, and little prize money. It was pretty much a band of fun-loving daredevils. Men such as

Swayne Pritchett, Fonty Flock, Red Byron, and Cotton Owens

raced the same kinds of cars their neighbors drove. A stock

car was originally a model right off the showroom floor, so

watching them race appealed to the average fan.

**These moonshiners must have used slower cars; rev-
enue agents move in to bust up crates of illegal liquor.**

THE FATHER OF NASCAR

One of the early stock car racers was William Henry Getty "Big Bill" France. He was an auto mechanic who had moved from Washington, D.C., to Daytona Beach in 1934. He loved the city's warm weather. He also loved the hard-sand beaches, which were ideal for high-speed driving.

France entered the first race there in 1936. Big Bill, who was 6 feet 5 inches (196 centimeters) and weighed 220 pounds (100 kilograms), was a pretty good driver. He enjoyed greater success, however, as one of a growing number of race organizers and promoters. He staged various races in Daytona and throughout the southeast over the next 10 years. In 1948, he founded NASCAR. He ruled the organization until 1972, when his son, William Jr., took over.

Bill France first made his mark as a driver, but his most lasting impact came off the track.

On December 14, 1947, William H. G. France held a historic meeting in Daytona Beach, Florida. Promoters, drivers, officials, and others involved in the growing yet disorganized sport gathered. "Big Bill" pitched the idea of forming one national group that would oversee stock car racing. This new group would also name an annual champion, based on points earned in competition. Two months later, on February 21, 1948, NASCAR became official, with France as its president. Its races that year were still a bit rag-tag. Drivers entered "modified" stock cars, with souped-up engines and specially rigged suspensions. Still, the stage was set for what would become America's most popular form of car racing.

Sand-churning races like this one on Daytona Beach in the 1940s were the forerunner of the colorful events of today.

C H A P T E R   T W O

Big Bill's Dream
Comes True

ill France believed the way to ensure NASCAR's popularity was to control what cars could race. He decided to ban modified cars from races and allowed only "strictly stock" models. He gathered a group of fearless, colorful drivers. He offered them a decent amount of prize money and the chance to compete for a national championship. France believed that fans would flock to cheer for their favorite drivers. The fans also would want to buy a car just like that driver. That was exactly what the nation's automakers needed to boost business. "Win on Sunday, sell on Monday," became a rallying cry.

Big Bill's dream was realized with the very first NASCAR

"strictly stock" race. It was a 150-mile (241-kilometer) thriller on June 19, 1949, at the 0.75-mile (1.2-kilometer) dirt track in Charlotte, North Carolina. A crowd of nearly 13,000 watched Glenn Dunnaway cross the finish line first. However, he was **disqualified** shortly afterward. His 1947 Ford had illegal springs boosting its rear end. Jim Roper, racing a 1949 Lincoln, was awarded the $2,000 first prize.

Seven more NASCAR races were staged that year, which ended with Red Byron capturing the first driver's champion-ship. That season also gave rise to some of the early legends of NASCAR. The top drivers included Lee Petty, the Flock brothers (Tim, Fonty, and Bob), Curtis Turner, and Herb

Big and fast, stock cars whiz by during the first official NASCAR event, held in Charlotte, North Carolina, in 1949.

Thomas. Other top racers were Buck Baker, Junior Johnson, Ned Jarrett, and Glenn "Fireball" Roberts. During the 1950s, they jostled each other on dirt and paved tracks up and down the East Coast.

Sticking to France's formula, they drove full-size stock cars. Their cars had names such as Hudson Hornet, Nash Ambassador, Olds 88, and Chrysler 300. The models were so similar to regular cars, many racers drove to the track in their race cars. This was before seat belts, roll bars, racing tires, and other safety features that are common today.

Junior Johnson was among NASCAR's first stars. He would go on to become a successful racing team owner, too.

NASCAR shifted to a higher gear in 1950 with the debut of a **superspeedway** in Darlington, South Carolina. It became the home of the Southern 500. On Labor Day, the 1.25-mile (2-kilometer) paved oval hosted a field of 75 cars. Few drivers anticipated the wear the track's high speeds caused to their tires. They also didn't expect to make so many pit stops for replacements. California driver Johnny Mantz wisely minimized his pit stops. He used heavy-duty truck tires

Ned Jarrett was a two-time NASCAR champ. His son Dale would also become a top driver in the 1990s.

instead of standard car tires and didn't have to stop as often as the other drivers. He took the **checkered flag** with an average speed of just more than 76 miles per hour (122 kilometers per hour).

The success of that first 500-miler helped start the Grand National Series, stock car racing's top division. That series would later become today's familiar **Winston Cup Series.** By 1955, NASCAR staged 175 events at more than 50 different racetracks. The decade closed on a spectacular note in 1959, with the unveiling of the sport's second superspeedway. It was located in Bill France's adopted home of Daytona Beach. That was also the year of the first Daytona 500, NASCAR's most important race. Johnny Beauchamp was declared the first winner. Several days later, a review of finish-line photos showed that Lee Petty had really won.

The controversy over that race fueled public interest in NASCAR. The sport continued to grow in popularity through the 1960s. More superspeedways opened and teams began to

SPEED

When Bill France arrived in Daytona Beach in 1934, the Florida city was already a hotbed for fast cars. In 1910, driver Barney Oldfield raced on the long, hard beach and set the one-mile speed record of 88.845 mph (142.951 kilometers per hour). By the 1930s, stock cars were racing on Daytona's renowned 4.1-mile (6.6-kilometer) Beach-Road Course. The cars zipped down Highway A1A for a stretch, then dodged waves along the beach. That gave way in 1959 to the Daytona International.

Johnny Beauchamp (73) battles Lee Petty in the first Daytona 500. After a photo review of the finish, Petty was declared the winner.

race more than one car. Highly trained **pit crews** were created. The cars themselves became more sophisticated and went faster.

Progress had its price, however. One sad moment came when Fireball Roberts died in a fiery crash in 1964. NASCAR had lost its first superstar. After the accident, many important safety measures were added. The most important was the new **nonflammable** gas tanks.

As old stars moved on, the next generation of hard-charging, crowd-pleasing drivers grew up. Fans cheered for drivers such as Richard Petty, David Pearson, Bobby Allison, and Cale Yarborough. Exciting times were about to roll.

18

Early NASCAR hero Fireball Roberts was killed in a 1964 accident during a race.

C H A P T E R   T H R E E

NASCAR Speeds Up

B y the 1970s, NASCAR was running on all cylinders. The circuit had loyal fans watching at first-class racetracks. The events were well organized. The cars were safer and the drivers more experienced. Corporate team **sponsors** and television entered the picture in this decade. They pumped money into the Winston Cup Series and beamed the sights and sounds into millions of living rooms.

There were great rivalries on the track. None proved more fierce or entertaining than the one between Richard Petty and David Pearson. Petty had been raised around race cars by his dad, Lee Petty, a three-time NASCAR champion. Richard loved being a sports celebrity. He always seemed happy to sign autographs and grant interviews. He worked hard to earn his nickname—"the King." Pearson was more reserved. He had also

grown up in the south around racing. However, he preferred life outside the spotlight. Both were skilled, bold, determined drivers. They regularly found themselves neck and neck at the finish line. Remarkably, the pair finished first and second together a record 63 times.

The two men locked horns in a classic duel at the 1976 Daytona 500. On the final lap, Petty's number 43 Dodge held a narrow lead over Pearson's number 21 Mercury. Pearson passed Petty, then on the last turn Petty tried to regain the lead. Petty bumped Pearson. The two cars first crashed into the outside wall before settling in the grassy infield. Pearson managed to steer his crumpled car back onto the track and barely captured the checkered flag. Petty couldn't restart his wreck, and he watched in frustration as Pearson won.

These types of weekly thrills and spills catapulted NASCAR

Duels in the sun: Richard Petty (43) and David Pearson often battled each other right to the checkered flag.

Sports television dates back to 1939, when a college baseball game aired on NBC. By the 1960s, baseball, football, basketball, and hockey were TV regulars. Not until 1979 was a NASCAR race first telecast from start to finish. The occasion was another nail-biting Daytona 500. Millions of American viewers sat glued to their sets as CBS followed the action. The race came down to a last-lap battle between Cale Yarborough and Donnie Allison. Running door-to-door, they bumped and smashed into the wall. Richard Petty motored to his sixth Daytona win. Yarborough, Allison, and his brother Bobby, however, wound up brawling in front of a national audience. Such dramatic action led to more NASCAR coverage on television. Today, every race is broadcast from green flag to checkered flag.

Bill Elliott's car shows how important sponsors became to race teams as NASCAR grew into a major sport.

into the 1980s. During that decade, another crop of talented young racers made their mark. Names like Dale "The Intimidator" Earnhardt, Darrell "Jaws" Waltrip, and "Million Dollar" Bill Elliott regularly made trips to Victory Lane.

However, great drivers in better and better cars soon went too far. In 1987, after Elliott rocketed his Ford up to 212 miles per hour (341 kilometers per hour), NASCAR slammed on the brakes. Officials required cars to install smaller **carburetors.** They also called for **restrictor plates** that limited horsepower. The goal has remained to keep speeds under 200 miles per hour (322 kilometers per hour).

The move hardly slowed down NASCAR's momentum, though. Instead, the drivers relied more on old-fashioned skills, guts, and the will to win. After all, that's what racing's all about. Fast doesn't always mean first.

The 1976 Daytona 500 ended with two bangs and a whimper. David Pearson (left) and Richard Petty both smashed their cars, but Pearson limped home the winner.

CHAPTER FOUR

Superspeedways and Superstars

NASCAR in the 1990s had come a long way since the early days when big cars whizzed around rutted dirt tracks. It was now big-time sports entertainment, right up there with other major sports.

NASCAR grew up mostly in the South, but its popularity had spread to every part of the country. Fans filled race tracks from Florida to California. Races were shown on TV every week, and NASCAR made front-page headlines in the sports pages. NASCAR caps, T-shirts, and souvenirs popped up in stores everywhere. NASCAR theme restaurants were

NASCAR events today are packed with fans from all over America.

opened, and an official Web site was created.

The decade saw even more changes to the sport. Sleeker, more aerodynamic cars were introduced to the Winston Cup circuit. Two of those were the Ford Taurus and Chevrolet Monte Carlo. New high-speed tracks were built in Los Angeles, Fort Worth, Las Vegas, and Miami. In 1995, NASCAR began its Craftsman Truck Series, races featuring powerful pickup trucks. Like the Busch Grand National Series, the trucks are a sort of racing minor league. The action is a little slower, allowing the drivers to hone their skills before graduat-

Today's tracks offer fans a great view of high-speed racing action, such as here at Martinsville, Virginia.

ing to the faster Winston Cup Series.

What hadn't changed, and probably never will, is the fans' love of the daring drivers. Fans still follow the veteran superstars and they look forward to exciting newcomers. A veteran and a rookie crossed paths at the 1992 Hooters 500 in Atlanta.

In the race, Richard Petty climbed into his familiar number 43 red-white-and-blue Pontiac. The beloved "King," then 55 years old, had won a record 200 Winston Cup races in his career. However, he hadn't finished first since 1984 in a race at Daytona. Earlier in 1992, he had announced that it would be his final season. In that Hooters race, the crowds still cheered when Petty finished in 16th place.

Farther back in the roaring pack in Atlanta was an unknown young man named Jeff Gordon. Raised in the San

The racing machines in the Craftsman Series are not your average pickup trucks; Busch Series cars are one step below Winston-level racers.

Francisco Bay area, Gordon moved to Indiana when he was 14. Gordon had a passion for racing from the time he first got behind the wheel of a go-kart at the age of three. Few people noticed when he finished 31st in that Hooters 500, well behind the King. Within just a few years, though, everyone knew the Boy Wonder of NASCAR.

Gordon was only 24 when he won his first Winston Cup championship in 1995. He would capture two more titles before the end of the decade. As the new millennium dawned, he had already established himself as one of NASCAR's greatest talents ever. To further prove the point, he won yet another championship in 2001. That season, however, was tarnished by a tragic accident at the fabled Daytona 500.

Dale Earnhardt came into the 2001 season with seven career Winston Cup titles. That total tied him with Richard Petty for the most ever. Even so, Earnhardt hadn't won the Daytona 500 until his 20th try in 1998. In 2001, he was in third

When he retired in 1992, Richard Petty could look back at a sport he helped build and a future that was bright indeed.

NOT FOR OVALS ONLY

Believe it or not, there are right-hand turns in NASCAR. Most of the race tracks are oval-shaped and steer to the left. There are two "road courses," however, that break the round-and-round mold. Like ovals, they feature straightaways and banking. The road courses also have S-curves and curves that bend over longer distances. In 1957, NASCAR began running at Watkins Glen, located in upstate New York. That twisting track is also home to the U.S. Formula One Grand Prix. It became a regular NASCAR stop in 1986. The other road course that stock car drivers tackle is in Sonoma, California. There, Sears Point Raceway winds drivers through 10 turns carved into the beautiful countryside.

All of a driver's skills are put to the test on twisting, turning road courses like this one at Sears Point in northern California.

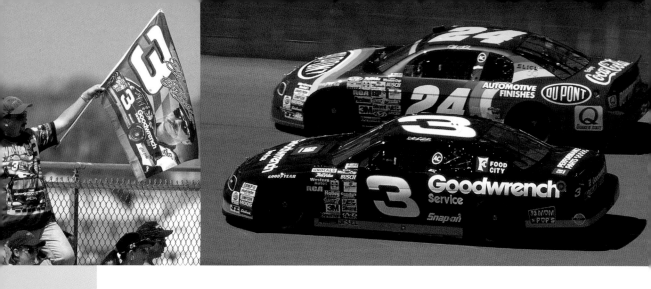

place on the final lap. Ahead of him, his son, Dale Jr., was battling with eventual winner Michael Waltrip for the lead. Suddenly, Earnhardt's black number 3 Chevy slammed head-on into the wall. The man they called "The Intimidator" was killed instantly. He was 49 years old.

The untimely death of one of NASCAR's best and most popular drivers was a terrible loss for fans and drivers. It was also a sad reminder of the danger of motor sports. The silver lining is that it forced NASCAR to look for ways to make racing safer for the future generations of drivers.

The future of NASCAR is bright. It has gone from dirt tracks in the South to a place among America's biggest sports. New drivers will come and go, but one thing will stay the same. The fans will call for speed—more speed!

The tragic death of Dale Earnhardt, No. 3, saddened millions of his fans. But the racing goes on in his memory.

NASCAR'S HISTORY

1947   William France Sr. meets with drivers, promoters and others in Daytona Beach, Florida, and they form NASCAR in 1948.

1949   NASCAR runs its first "strictly stock" race, a 150-mile contest at Charlotte, North Carolina, won by Jim Roper.

1950   NASCAR unveils its first paved track, the Darlington Raceway in South Carolina.

1959   The first-ever Daytona 500 is run at the new Daytona International Speedway; the winner is Lee Petty.

1971   R. J. Reynolds Co. signs an agreement with NASCAR to sponsor the Winston Cup Series

1976   ABC televises the dramatic conclusion of the Daytona 500. On the last lap, Richard Petty bumps rival David Pearson. They both spin into the infield, but Pearson wins.

1979   The first NASCAR race shown flag-to-flag on TV, the Daytona 500, ends with a crash. Drivers Cale Yarborough and the Allison brothers, Bobby and Donnie, then start a brawl on the infield.

1992   Richard Petty competes in his final Winston Cup race.

1997   Jeff Gordon, at age 26, is the youngest driver ever to win the Daytona 500. He also captures his second Winston Cup title.

1998   On his 20th try, Dale Earnhardt finally wins the Daytona 500.

2001   Seven-time Winston Cup champion Dale Earnhardt crashes on the last lap of the Daytona 500. His car hits a wall and he is killed. Jeff Gordon captures his fourth Winston Cup title.

GLOSSARY

carburetors—the part of the engine that mixes air and fuel to create small explosions; these explosions move pistons up and down that make the engine run.

checkered flag—the black-and-white flag waved at the winner of a race as he crosses the finish line

disqualified—to be removed from a race or race results for breaking the rules

Grand Prix—former name of international racing circuit that uses open-wheel cars; today the circuit is called "Formula 1."

nonflammable—fireproof

pit crews—the teams that service cars during races with gas and tires; they work in special "pit" areas alongside the track.

restrictor plates—A device put on a race car's carburetor to reduce horsepower and speed

sponsors—companies or individuals who put up money to help race teams

superspeedway—a paved, oval race track, 1 mile (1.6 kilometers) or longer, with high-banked curves

Winston Cup Series—NASCAR's top circuit of races, for which drivers earn points toward an annual national championship; other NASCAR circuits include the Busch Grand National Series and Craftsman Truck Series.

TO LEARN MORE ABOUT NASCAR AND ITS HISTORY

Books

Center, Bill. *Ultimate Stock Car.* New York: Dorling Kindersley, 2000.

McGuire, Ann. *The History of NASCAR.* Broomall, Penn.: Chelsea House Publishers, 2000.

Menzer, Joe. *The Wildest Ride.* New York: Simon & Schuster, 2001.

Owens, Thomas S., and Diana Star Helmer. *NASCAR.* New York: Twenty-First Century Books, 2000.

Web Sites

The Official NASCAR Web Site
http://www.NASCAR.com
For an overview of an entire season of NASCAR as well as the history of the sport and a dictionary of racing terms

Motor Sports
http://www.msnbc.com/news/MOTORSPORTS
A combined site produced by NBC Sports, MSNBC, and *The Sporting News*

Fox Sports Network
http://www.foxsports.com
Click on the checkered flag, then NASCAR to find more details

ESPN
http://www.espn.com
The all-sports cable network has a special racing area called rpm.espn.com

INDEX

ABOUT THE AUTHOR

Bob Woods is a freelance writer in Madison, Connecticut. Over the past 27 years, his work has appeared in numerous magazines, including *Sports Illustrated, Newsweek International, Continental*, and *Chief Executive.* He has written sports biographies for young readers about Ken Griffey Jr., Barry Bonds, and Shaquille O'Neal.